All-Time Favorite

Banana

Recipes

DALMATIAN PRESS

With very special thanks to
the Dole Food Company
for its scrumptious collection of
favorite banana recipes
and photographs.

ALL-TIME FAVORITE BANANA RECIPES
Copyright © 2005 Dalmatian Press, LLC

Recipes, photographs, and nutritional facts are
copyright © Dole Food Company, Inc., used by permission.
Banana pudding recipe and photograph
copyright © 2005 Dalmatian Press, LLC

Design by Melissa Dickson Orum
Cover photograph by KnightVision Photography

The DALMATIAN PRESS name is a trademark of
Dalmatian Press, LLC, Franklin, Tennessee 37067.
The DOLE name and logo are trademarks of Dole Food Company. Inc.

ISBN: 1-40371-338-3 (X)
1-40371-337-5 (M)
13967-0305

05 06 07 08 QWB 10 9 8 7 6 5 4 3 2 1

Table of Contents

Banana Blueberry Coffee Ring

½ cup slivered almonds
3 medium, ripe DOLE®
    Bananas
½ cup softened margarine
1 cup sugar
1 egg
¼ cup sour cream

1¾ cup all-purpose flour
2 teaspoons baking powder
1 teaspoon ground
    cinnamon
¼ teaspoon ground nutmeg
1 cup fresh or frozen
    blueberries

Grease and flour 10-inch tube pan. Sprinkle almonds over bottom of pan; set aside.

Place bananas in food processor or blender container.

Cover and blend until smooth. Measure 1½ cups mashed bananas into large bowl.

Add margarine, sugar, egg and sour cream to bananas; beat until well blended.

Stir together flour, baking powder, cinnamon and nutmeg in medium bowl. Add to banana mixture, with blueberries, until just blended. Pour into prepared pan.

Bake at 350°F 40 to 45 minutes or until toothpick inserted in center comes out clean. Cool in pan 10 minutes; turn onto wire rack to cool. Serve warm or at room temperature.

Prep: 20 minutes   Bake: 45 minutes   Makes: 12 servings

Per Serving: 277 calories, 12g fat (2g sat.), 19mg cholesterol, 137mg sodium,
40g carbohydrate (2g dietary fiber, 21g sugars), 4g protein, 8% Vit A,
6% Vit C, 4% calcium, 4% iron, 5% potassium, 4% folate

What makes bananas sweet? Natural starches in the fruit that gradually turn to sugar. The riper the banana, the sweeter the taste.

Springtime Waffles

2 small DOLE® Bananas
¾ cup sliced strawberries
⅓ cup 100% strawberry fruit spread
1 teaspoon grated lemon peel
4 frozen waffles

Thinly slice bananas. Mix bananas, strawberries, strawberry fruit spread and lemon peel.

Prepare waffles according to package directions. Spoon banana strawberry sauce over waffles to serve.

Prep: 15 minutes   Makes: 2 servings

Per Serving: 404 calories, 6g fat (1g sat.), 22mg cholesterol, 525mg sodium, 85g carbohydrate (6g dietary fiber, 41g sugars), 6g protein, 19% Vit A, 72% Vit C, 17 % calcium, 20% iron, 17% potassium, 20% folate

Quick Breakfast Rolls

¼ **cup sliced almonds, toasted**
½ **cup packed brown sugar**
1 **teaspoon ground cinnamon**
½ **teaspoon ground nutmeg**
4 **tablespoons margarine, divided**
1 **ripe, large DOLE® Banana, chopped**
1 **pkg. (8 oz.) refrigerator crescent rolls**

Combine almonds, brown sugar, cinnamon and nutmeg in small bowl. Spray muffin pan with vegetable cooking spray.
Place 1 teaspoon margarine and 1 tablespoon sugar mixture in each prepared muffin cup.
Add banana to remaining sugar mixture. Unroll crescent dough from package and pinch seams together. Spread banana mixture over dough. Roll up from long side. Cut into 12 pieces and place each spiral into a muffin cup.
Bake at 375°F 20 to 25 minutes. Loosen edges; invert pan onto serving plate. Serve while warm with fresh orange wedges, grapes and strawberries, if desired.

Prep: 20 minutes   Bake: 20 minutes   Makes: 12 servings

Per Serving: 169 calories, 9g fat (2g sat.), 0mg cholesterol, 264mg sodium,
21g carbohydrate (1g dietary fiber, 10g sugars), 2g protein, 4% Vit A,
2% Vit C, 3% calcium, 5% iron, 4% potassium, 4% folate

Banana Brunch Coffee Cake

2 ripe, medium DOLE®
   Bananas
1 standard pkg. yellow
   cake mix
1 small box instant
   vanilla pudding mix
½ cup vegetable oil

4 eggs
1 teaspoon vanilla extract
½ cup chopped almonds
⅓ cup packed brown sugar
1 teaspoon ground cinnamon
½ teaspoon ground nutmeg

Puree bananas in blender (1 cup). Combine bananas, cake
mix, pudding mix, oil, eggs and vanilla in large mixing bowl.
Mix well and beat at medium speed 8 minutes, scraping
sides of bowl occasionally.

Combine almonds, brown sugar, cinnamon and nutmeg.
Pour one-half cake batter into greased 3-quart Bundt pan.
Sprinkle with sugar mixture. Cover with remaining batter.
Insert knife in batter and swirl in figure-eight patterns
through layers. (Be sure not to overmix the layers.)

Bake at 325°F 60 to 65 minutes. Cool in pan on wire
rack 10 minutes. Invert onto rack to complete cooling.
Dust with powdered sugar when cool, and garnish with
sliced bananas, raspberries and fresh mint, if desired.

Prep: 15 minutes   Bake: 60 minutes   Makes: 12 servings

Per Serving: 388 calories, 18g fat (2g sat.), 71mg cholesterol, 433mg sodium,
53g carbohydrate (2g dietary fiber, 16g sugars), 5g protein, 2% Vit A, 3% Vit C,
9% calcium, 5% iron, 5% potassium, 4% folate

Banana Raisin Pancakes

2 extra-ripe, medium
DOLE® Bananas
1 egg, slightly beaten
¾ cup low-fat milk

1 tablespoon vegetable oil
1 cup pancake mix
½ cup seedless raisins
⅛ teaspoon ground cinnamon

Mash bananas (1 cup). Combine bananas, egg, milk and oil.
Combine pancake mix, raisins and cinnamon. Stir into
banana mixture until just moistened.
Pour ¼ cup batter onto lightly greased hot skillet for each
pancake. Brown on underside until bubbles appear on sur-
face. Turn and brown other side.

Prep: 15 minutes   Cook: 20 minutes   Makes: 6 servings

Per Serving: 306 calories, 7g fat (1g sat.), 63mg cholesterol, 394mg sodium,
55g carbohydrate (3g dietary fiber, 29g sugars), 7g protein, 4% Vit A, 9% Vit C,
17% calcium, 11% iron, 14% potassium, 13% folate

Tropical Blueberry Smoothie

1 can (8 oz.) crushed pineapple, drained
1 ripe DOLE® Banana, sliced
1 cup milk
1 cup frozen blueberries

Combine crushed pineapple, banana, milk and blueberries in blender or food processor container. Cover; blend until thick and smooth. Serve immediately. Garnish with banana, strawberry, mint kabob, if desired.

Prep: 10 minutes   Makes: 3 servings

Per Serving: 142 calories, 3g fat (2g sat.), 8mg cholesterol, 36mg sodium, 28g carbohydrate (3g dietary fiber, 21g sugars), 4g protein, 3% Vit A, 22% Vit C, 9% calcium, 2% iron, 10% potassium, 4% folate

Island Shake

1 medium, ripe DOLE® Banana
1 ripe mango, cubed
1 cup pineapple juice
½ cup low-fat peach yogurt
½ cup ice cubes
½ teaspoon finely grated lemon peel

Combine banana, mango, pineapple juice, yogurt, ice and lemon peel in blender or food processor container. Cover; blend until thick and smooth. Garnish with orange wedge and banana slice, if desired.

Prep: 10 minutes   Makes: 3 servings

Per Serving: 163 calories, 1g fat (0g sat.), 2mg cholesterol, 27mg sodium, 39g carbohydrate (2g dietary fiber, 33g sugars), 3g protein, 12% Vit A, 53% Vit C, 7% calcium, 2% iron, 13% potassium, 9% folate

Banana Raspberry Smoothie

1½ cups pineapple juice
1 cup vanilla low-fat yogurt
    or frozen yogurt
1 cup frozen raspberries
2 ripe, medium DOLE® Bananas

Combine pineapple juice, yogurt, raspberries and bananas in blender or food processor container. Cover; blend until smooth. Garnish with banana slices.

Prep: 10 minutes   Makes 3 servings

Per Serving: 231 calories, 2g fat (1g sat.), 4mg cholesterol, 56mg sodium, 51g carbohydrate (5g dietary fiber, 40g sugars), 6g protein, 2% Vit A, 53% Vit C, 18% calcium, 5% iron, 20% potassium, 16% folate

Paradise Freeze

1 large, ripe DOLE® Banana
1 cup strawberries
1 ripe mango, cubed
1 cup cranberry juice
1 cup ice cubes

Combine banana, strawberries, mango, cranberry juice and ice in blender or food processor container. Cover; blend until thick and smooth.

 **Prep: 10 minutes   Makes: 3 servings**

Per Serving: 143 calories, 1g fat (0g sat.), 0mg cholesterol, 4mg sodium, 37g carbohydrate (3g dietary fiber, 29g sugars), 1g protein, 11% Vit A, 134% Vit C, 2% calcium, 3% iron, 10% potassium, 7% folate

Banana Honey Shake

2 medium, ripe DOLE®
Bananas, quartered
½ cup non-fat milk
2 tablespoons honey
Ground nutmeg (optional)

Combine bananas, milk and honey in blender or food processor container. Cover; blend until thick and smooth. Pour into serving glass or container. Sprinkle with nutmeg, if desired.

 **Prep: 5 minutes   Makes: 1 serving**

Per Serving: 220 calories, 2g fat (1g sat.), 6mg cholesterol, 63mg sodium, 50g carbohydrate (3g dietary fiber, 38g sugars), 5g protein, 6% Vit A, 17% Vit C, 14% calcium, 5% iron, 17% potassium, 8% folate

Chocolate Banana Peanut Butter Shake

1 cup low-fat chocolate milk or
low-fat chocolate soy beverage
1 medium ripe DOLE® Banana
¼ cup creamy peanut butter
1 tablespoon honey
6 ice cubes

Combine milk, bananas, peanut butter, honey and ice cubes in blender or food processer container. Cover; blend until smooth. Pour into glasses and serve immediately.

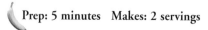 **Prep: 5 minutes   Makes: 2 servings**

Per Serving: 258 calories, 10g fat (2g sat.), 6mg cholesterol, 149mg sodium, 37g carbohydrate (3g dietary fiber, 28g sugars), 9g protein, 6% Vit A, 9% Vit C, 14% calcium, 6% iron, 13% potassium, 8% folate

Teriyaki Fruit and Rice Salad

¼ cup light soy sauce
¼ cup packed brown sugar
1 teaspoon molasses
½ teaspoon grated
   fresh ginger
½ teaspoon cornstarch
1 tablespoon water
1 large DOLE® Banana, sliced

4 cups cooked white rice,
   cooled
1 cup snow peas, trimmed,
   cut in thirds
¼ cup chopped
   dried apricots
¼ cup slivered almonds,
   toasted
1 teaspoon sesame oil

Stir together soy sauce, brown sugar, molasses and ginger in small saucepan. Dissolve cornstarch in water in small cup or bowl; stir into mixture. Cook, stirring until mixture boils and slightly thickens. Cool.

Combine banana, rice, snow peas, apricots, almonds and sesame oil in large bowl. Pour cooled dressing over salad. Toss to evenly coat.

Prep: 20 minutes   Cook: 5 minutes   Makes: 4 servings

Per Serving: 427 calories, 6g fat (1g sat.), 0mg cholesterol, 518mg sodium,
85g carbohydrate (3g dietary fiber, 25g sugars), 9g protein, 6% Vit A,
20% Vit C, 6% calcium, 23% iron, 12% potassium, 31% folate

Bananas stir up tasty dishes with good nutrition.
Just one banana provides 16% of the fiber, 15%
of the vitamin C and 11% of the potassium that
we need every day for good health.

Honey Lime Fruit Toss

1 can (20 oz.) pineapple chunks
1 can (11 or 15 oz.) Mandarin oranges, drained
1 large DOLE® Banana, sliced
1 kiwi fruit, peeled, halved and sliced
1 cup quartered strawberries
¼ teaspoon grated lime peel (optional)
2 tablespoons fresh lime juice
1 tablespoon honey

Drain pineapple; reserve ¼ cup juice. In large serving bowl combine pineapple chunks, mandarin oranges, banana, kiwi fruit and strawberries.

Stir together reserved pineapple juice, lime peel, lime juice and honey in small bowl. Pour over salad; toss to coat.

Prep: 10 minutes   Makes: 7 servings

Per Serving: 103 calories, 0g fat (0g sat.), 0mg cholesterol, 3mg sodium, 26g carbohydrate (2g dietary fiber, 22g sugars), 1g protein, 5% Vit A, 62% Vit C, 2% calcium, 3% iron, 7% potassium, 3% folate

Tropical Waldorf Salad

2 firm, large DOLE® Bananas,
  sliced
2 large, tart apples, cored,
  sliced
1 cup diced celery
½ cup chopped dates
½ cup chopped walnuts

½ cup mayonnaise
2 tablespoons sour cream
1 teaspoon lemon juice
⅛ teaspoon ground ginger
Crisp salad greens
¼ cup flaked coconut
  (optional)

Combine bananas, apples, celery, dates and walnuts in large bowl.

Stir together mayonnaise, sour cream, lemon juice and ginger. Pour over fruit and toss. Serve on salad greens. Sprinkle with coconut, if desired.

 **Prep: 15 minutes   Makes: 6 servings**

Per Serving: 312 calories, 22g fat (3g sat.), 15mg cholesterol, 134mg sodium,
29g carbohydrate (4g dietary fiber, 20g sugars), 3g protein, 2% Vit A,
13% Vit C, 3% calcium, 4% iron, 11% potassium, 7% folate

Caribbean Caesar Salad

2 Romaine hearts,
  torn into pieces
2 cups fresh pineapple,
  cut into chunks
1 cup mango, peeled,
  sliced

3 boneless, skinless,
  chicken breast halves
1 DOLE® Banana, sliced
4 teaspoons lime juice
⅓ cup fat-free or regular
  Caesar dressing

Toss together romaine, pineapple chunks and mango in bowl.
Broil or grill chicken breasts 15 to 20 minutes or until meat is no longer pink in center. Slice chicken and place on salad with bananas.
Stir lime juice and dressing, until blended, in small bowl. Drizzle over chicken and salad.

Prep: 15 minutes   Grill: 20 minutes   Makes: 3 servings

Per Serving: 468 calories, 20g fat (4g sat.), 97mg cholesterol, 375mg sodium,
37g carbohydrate (4g dietary fiber, 26g sugars), 38g protein, 43% Vit A,
127% Vit C, 7% calcium, 13% iron, 19% potassium, 10% folate

Calypso Black Bean and Fruit Salad

1 can (15 oz.) reduced sodium
   black beans, drained

3 tablespoons prepared salsa

2 tablespoons chopped
   fresh cilantro

1 tablespoon finely chopped
   red onion

½ teaspoon grated orange peel

1 tablespoon lime juice

¼ teaspoon ground cumin

1 large DOLE® Banana, sliced

1 orange, sectioned

Red leaf lettuce (optional)

1 oz. feta cheese,
   crumbled (optional)

Combine beans, salsa, cilantro, onion, orange peel, lime
juice and cumin in medium bowl. Gently stir in banana
and orange. Spoon onto lettuce-lined, small serving platter.
Sprinkle cheese on top of salad, if desired. Squeeze addi-
tional lime juice over bananas.

Prep: 15 minutes   Makes: 4 servings

Per Serving: 124 calories, 2g fat (1g sat.), 6mg cholesterol, 324mg sodium,
26g carbohydrate (7g dietary fiber, 8g sugars), 6g protein, 6% Vit A, 42%
Vit C, 9% calcium, 10% iron, 14% potassium, 5% folate

Baker Beach Salad

3 cups fresh spinach
1 DOLE® Banana, sliced
½ cup raspberries or 1 orange, peeled, sliced
½ cup sliced radishes or cucumber
½ cup slivered carrots
6 oz. barbecued or smoked deli chicken, sliced
1 tablespoon grated Parmesan cheese (optional)
¼ cup fat-free or reduced-calorie Italian salad dressing

Place spinach on two salad plates. Arrange banana, raspberries, radishes, carrots and chicken over spinach. Sprinkle Parmesan cheese over each serving, if desired. Pour dressing over salads.

Prep: 15 minutes   Makes: 2 servings

Per Serving: 281 calories, 7g fat (3g sat.), 21mg cholesterol, 1123mg sodium, 44g carbohydrate (9g dietary fiber, 16g sugars), 12g protein, 121% Vit A, 52% Vit C, 17% calcium, 28% iron, 18% potassium, 8% folate

Ambrosia Banana Muffins

2 extra-ripe, medium DOLE®
 Bananas
⅓ cup milk
¼ cup vegetable oil
1 egg, beaten
2 cups all-purpose flour
⅓ cup sugar
1 tablespoon baking powder
1 teaspoon grated orange peel

½ teaspoon ground allspice
¼ teaspoon salt
¾ cup chopped dates
½ cup chopped pecans
2 tablespoons minced
 crystallized ginger
½ cup shredded coconut
 (optional)

Place bananas in blender or food processor container. Cover; blend until smooth (1 cup). Add milk, oil and egg. Blend again.

Combine flour, sugar, baking powder, orange peel, allspice, salt and dates in large bowl. Make well in center. Stir in banana mixture, just until blended. Fill 12 paper-lined muffin cups two-thirds full.

Combine nuts and ginger; sprinkle over muffins, pressing in gently. Shredded coconut optional.

Bake at 375°F 20 to 25 minutes or until toothpick inserted in center comes out clean. Let stand 5 minutes.

Prep: 20 minutes   Bake: 15 minutes   Makes: 12 muffins

Per Serving: 229 calories, 9g fat (1g sat.), 18mg cholesterol, 121mg sodium, 36g carbohydrate (2g dietary fiber, 16g sugars), 4g protein, 1% Vit A, 3% Vit C, 4% calcium, 7% iron, 5% potassium, 11% folate

The best way to store bananas isn't in a bowl or a basket. A banana hanger or hook will help preserve the quality of a ripe banana and prevent "resting bruises."

Banana Blueberry Muffins

2 ripe, medium
   DOLE® Bananas
2 eggs
1 cup packed brown sugar
½ cup margarine, melted
1 cup fresh or frozen
   blueberries

1 teaspoon vanilla extract
1 teaspoon grated lemon peel
2¼ cups all-purpose flour
2 teaspoons baking powder
½ teaspoon ground
   cinnamon
½ teaspoon salt

Place bananas in blender or food processor container.
Cover; blend until smooth (1 cup).

Combine bananas, eggs, sugar and margarine until well
blended in medium bowl. Stir in blueberries, vanilla and
lemon peel.

Stir together flour, baking powder, cinnamon and salt in
large bowl. Make a well in center of dry ingredients. Add
liquid mixture. Mix until just blended. Spoon batter into
greased muffin cups.

Bake at 350°F 25 to 30 minutes or until toothpick comes
out clean.

Prep: 15 minutes   Bake: 30 minutes   Makes: 12 muffins

Per Serving: 169 calories, 1g fat (0g sat.), 35mg cholesterol, 154mg sodium,
36g carbohydrate (2g dietary fiber, 16g sugars), 4g protein, 1% Vit A, 5% Vit C,
35% calcium, 2% iron, 5% potassium, 13% folate

Banana Lemon Bread

2 extra-ripe, medium
DOLE® Bananas
¼ cup margarine, melted
2 cups all-purpose flour
1 teaspoon baking powder
½ teaspoon baking soda
½ teaspoon salt

1 egg
¼ cup sugar
1 tablespoon grated
lemon peel
⅓ cup lemon juice
⅓ cup sugar

Place quartered bananas into blender or food processor container. Cover; blend until smooth. Stir in margarine.

Combine flour, baking powder, baking soda and salt; set aside. Beat egg, ¼ cup sugar and lemon peel in large bowl. Add bananas and blend. Beat in flour mixture. Pour batter into 9x5-inch loaf pan coated with vegetable cooking spray.

Bake at 350°F 35 minutes or until toothpick inserted in center comes out clean. Cool in pan. Poke holes in bread with skewer.

Stir together lemon juice and ⅓ cup sugar in small saucepan. Heat to boiling for 1 minute.

Pour lemon syrup over bread. Let stand 10 minutes; remove from pan.

Prep: 15 minutes   Bake: 35 minutes   Makes: 12 servings

Per Serving: 171 calories, 4g fat (1g sat.), 18mg cholesterol, 220mg sodium, 30g carbohydrate (1g dietary fiber, 12g sugars), 3g protein, 4% Vit A, 9% Vit C, 2% calcium, 6% iron, 3% potassium, 11% folate

Banana Muffins

2 extra-ripe, medium
   DOLE® Bananas
1 egg
⅔ cup packed brown sugar
⅓ cup buttermilk
⅓ cup vegetable oil
1 teaspoon vanilla extract

1¼ cups all-purpose flour
½ cup whole wheat flour
2 teaspoons baking powder
1 teaspoon ground nutmeg
½ teaspoon baking soda
¼ teaspoon salt

Puree bananas in blender container (1 cup). Beat egg and sugar until smooth, in medium bowl. Mix in pureed bananas, buttermilk, oil and vanilla.

Combine flours, baking powder, nutmeg, baking soda and salt in medium bowl; stir into banana mixture, mixing just to blend. Spoon into greased or paper-lined muffin cups.

Bake at 375°F 17 to 20 minutes or until wooden pick inserted in center comes out clean. Turn out onto racks to cool.

Prep: 15 minutes   Bake: 20 minutes   Makes: 12 muffins

Per Serving: 191 calories, 7g fat (1g sat.), 18mg cholesterol, 180mg sodium, 31g carbohydrate (2g dietary fiber, 15g sugars), 3g protein, 1% Vit A, 3% Vit C, 8% calcium, 4% iron, 5% potassium, 3% folate

Cocoa Raisin Muffins

2 very ripe, medium
    DOLE® Bananas
1 egg, beaten
⅓ cup vegetable oil
1 teaspoon vanilla extract
1½ cups all-purpose flour

1 cup sugar
6 tablespoons cocoa powder
1 teaspoon baking soda
½ teaspoon salt
¼ teaspoon baking powder
½ cup seedless raisins

Put bananas into food processor bowl or blender. Secure lid and blend until smooth. Scrape banana into a mixing bowl and combine with egg and oil. In another mixing bowl, combine flour, sugar, cocoa, baking soda, salt and baking powder. Add banana mixture, and stir until moistened. Stir in raisins. Spoon batter into greased muffin cups or loaf pan.

Bake at 350°F —

        mini muffins: 12 to 15 minutes
        regular muffins: 20 to 25 minutes
        loaf: 55 to 60 minutes; cool completely to slice

Prep: 20 minutes   **Bake:** 15 minutes   **Makes:** 48 mini muffins

Per Serving: 187calories, 5g fat (1g sat.), 0mg cholesterol, 243mg sodium,
32g carbohydrate (2g dietary fiber, 13g sugars), 4g protein, 51% Vit A,
8% Vit C, 4% calcium, 9% iron, 6% potassium, 12% folate

Banana Tot Pops

3 firm, medium DOLE® Bananas
6 large wooden pop sticks
¾ cup raspberry or other flavored yogurt
1 jar (1.75 oz.) chocolate or rainbow sprinkles

Cut each banana crosswise in half. Insert wooden stick into each half.

Pour yogurt on luncheon plate. Roll bananas in yogurt. Allow excess yogurt to drip onto plate. Sprinkle candies over yogurt.

Place pops on wax paper-lined tray. Freeze 2 hours.

Prep: 20 minutes   Freeze: 2 hours   Makes: 6 servings

Per Serving: 125 calories, 2g fat (2g sat.), 1mg cholesterol, 21mg sodium, 25g carbohydrate (2g dietary fiber, 13g sugars), 2g protein, 1% Vit A, 9% Vit C, 6% calcium, 4% iron, 9% potassium, 4% folate

Chunky Banana Spread

1 package (8 oz.) fat-free cream cheese, softened
2 ripe DOLE® Bananas
1 tablespoon lemon juice
¼ cup chopped dried apricots
¾ teaspoon ground cinnamon
¼ teaspoon ground ginger
Chopped almonds (optional)
Toasted bagels or crackers

Mix together cream cheese, bananas and lemon juice in mixing bowl until smooth. Stir in apricots, cinnamon and ginger. Garnish with chopped almonds, dried apricots and banana slice, if desired. Spread on toasted bagels or crackers.

Prep: 15 minutes   Makes: 8 servings or 2 cups

Per Serving: 65 calories, 1g fat (0g sat.), 2mg cholesterol, 155mg sodium, 11g carbohydrate (1g dietary fiber, 6g sugars), 5g protein, 9% Vit A, 6 % Vit C, 6% calcium, 2% iron, 6% potassium, 4% folate

Banana S'mores

1 firm DOLE® Banana, sliced
12 graham cracker squares
6 large marshmallows
1 bar (1.55 oz.) milk chocolate candy

Arrange 4 banana slices on each of 6 graham cracker squares. Top each one with a marshmallow. Microwave 12 to 15 seconds or until puffed.

Place 2 squares chocolate on remaining 6 graham crackers. Microwave 1 minute or until just soft. Combine halves to make sandwiches.

Prep: 5 minutes   Microwave: 1 minute   Makes: 6 servings

Per Serving: 139 calories, 4g fat (2g sat.), 2mg cholesterol, 98mg sodium, 25g carbohydrate (1g dietary fiber, 15g sugars), 2g protein, 1% Vit A, 3% Vit C, 2% calcium, 4% iron, 3% potassium, 3% folate

Choco-Banana Bites

1 cup hot fudge topping
4 green-tipped DOLE® Bananas
Chopped toasted almonds for topping
Chopped butter brickle candy for topping
Decorative sprinkles for topping

Place hot fudge topping in 9-inch glass pie plate. Microwave on HIGH for 45 seconds or until thin consistency.

Cut each banana into 4 pieces. Place banana pieces in warm sauce. Using two forks, turn to coat with chocolate.

Roll in topping of choice. Place on wax paper on small plate. Repeat process, coating all bananas.

Freeze bananas for 30 minutes. Defrost slightly and serve.

Prep: 20 minutes   Freeze: 2 hours   Makes: 6 servings

Per Serving: 412 calories, 14g fat (4g sat.), 5mg cholesterol, 361mg sodium,
69g carbohydrate (5g dietary fiber, 45g sugars), 7g protein, 2% Vit A,
17% Vit C, 11% calcium, 4% iron, 20% potassium, 6% folate

Banana Energy Balls

1 extra-ripe, medium DOLE® Banana	2 tablespoons honey
¼ cup peanut butter	1⅓ cups natural wheat and barley cereal
¼ cup chocolate chips	⅓ cup finely chopped peanuts

Mash banana (½ cup).

Combine banana, peanut butter and chocolate chips.

Heat honey in microwave on HIGH for 15 seconds or until hot. Add to banana mixture; stir 30 seconds. Add cereal; mix well. Cover; set aside for 30 minutes.

Form balls using 1 tablespoon mixture, then roll in peanuts. Store in airtight container.

Prep: 25 minutes   Chill: 30 minutes   Makes: 20 bars

Per Serving: 60 calories, 3g fat (1g sat.), 0mg cholesterol, 48mg sodium,
8g carbohydrate (1g dietary fiber, 5g sugars), 2g protein, 1% Vit A,
10 % Vit C, 9% calcium, 10% iron, 2% potassium, 10% folate

Banana Holiday Cookies

2¾ cups all-purpose flour
1 teaspoon baking soda
¼ teaspoon salt
1 cup margarine, softened
1¼ cups granulated sugar, divided

¼ cup packed brown sugar
1 egg
1 large, ripe DOLE® Banana, mashed (½ cup)
½ teaspoon ground cinnamon

Combine flour, baking soda and salt in bowl; set aside.
Beat together margarine, 1 cup granulated sugar and brown sugar in large bowl until light and fluffy. Beat in egg and banana until blended. Stir in flour mixture until combined. Cover and refrigerate 2 hours or overnight until dough is firm enough to handle.
Combine remaining ¼ cup granulated sugar and cinnamon in small bowl.
Shape dough into 1-inch balls. Roll in cinnamon mixture; place 2 inches apart on ungreased baking sheets.
Bake at 350°F 10 to 12 minutes or until lightly browned. Carefully place cookies on wire rack to cool completely.

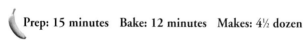 **Prep: 15 minutes   Bake: 12 minutes   Makes: 4½ dozen**

Per Serving: 61 calories, 4g fat (1g sat.), 4mg cholesterol, 75mg sodium, 7g carbohydrate (0g dietary fiber, 1g sugars), 1g protein, 3% Vit A, 0% Vit C, 0% calcium, 2% iron, 1% potassium, 3% folate

Variations:

Chocolate Banana Stars: Prepare, shape and bake dough as directed except roll dough in 1 cup finely chopped almonds instead of cinnamon mixture. Immediately after baking, press an unwrapped individual milk chocolate piece into center of each cookie. Cool as directed.
Banana Chippers: Prepare and shape dough as directed except stir in 1 package (10 oz.) peanut butter chips and 1 cup chopped pecans or walnuts into dough and omit cinnamon mixture. Bake and cool as directed above.
Zana Kringles: Stir 1 teaspoon ground ginger into flour mixture and replace brown sugar with 2 tablespoons molasses. Prepare, shape, bake and cool as directed.

Banana Oatmeal Raisin Cookies

2 extra-ripe, medium DOLE® Bananas
¾ cup light margarine
¾ cup packed brown sugar
1 egg
½ teaspoon vanilla extract
1½ cups quick-cooking oats

1½ cups all-purpose flour
1 teaspoon ground cinnamon
½ teaspoon baking soda
½ teaspoon salt
1½ cups seedless raisins
Vegetable cooking spray

Puree bananas in blender (1 cup).

Beat margarine and sugar. Beat in egg, then mashed bananas and vanilla.

Combine oats, flour, cinnamon, baking soda and salt; stir into banana mixture, just until blended. Mix in raisins.

Drop by rounded tablespoonfuls 2 inches apart on baking sheets sprayed with vegetable cooking spray. Flatten tops with back of spoon.

Bake at 350°F 12 to 15 minutes or until lightly browned.

Prep: 15 minutes   Bake: 15 minutes   Makes: 24 cookies

Per Serving: 146 calories, 4g fat (1g sat.), 9mg cholesterol, 127mg sodium, 27g carbohydrate (1g dietary fiber, 13g sugars), 2g protein, 0 % Vit A, 2% Vit C, 2% calcium, 6% iron, 4% potassium, 4 % folate

Double Chocolate Banana Cookies

3 to 4 extra-ripe, medium
   DOLE® Bananas
2 cups rolled oats
2 cups sugar
1¾ cups all-purpose flour
½ cup unsweetened cocoa
   powder
1 teaspoon baking soda

½ teaspoon salt
2 eggs, slightly beaten
1¼ cups margarine, melted
1 cup chopped almonds,
   toasted
2 cups semisweet
   chocolate chips

Cut bananas into quarters and place in blender or food processor container. Cover; blend until mashed. Measure 2 cups for recipe.

Combine oats, sugar, flour, cocoa, baking soda and salt in medium bowl until well mixed. Stir in bananas, eggs and margarine until blended. Add almonds and chocolate chips.

Cover and refrigerate batter 1 hour or until mixture becomes partially firm. (Batter becomes runny during baking if too soft). Drop by heaping tablespoonfuls onto greased cookie sheets.

Bake at 350°F 10 to 15 minutes or until cookies are dry to the touch. Remove to wire rack to cool.

Prep: 15 minutes   Chill: 1 hour
Bake: 17 minutes   Makes: 6½ dozen

Per Serving: 101 calories, 5g fat (2g sat.), 5mg cholesterol, 68mg sodium,
13g carbohydrate (1g dietary fiber, 8g sugars), 1g protein, 3% Vit A,
1% Vit C, 1% calcium, 3% iron, 2% potassium, 2% folate

Banana Peanut Butter Cookies

1 large ripe DOLE® Banana	1 egg
⅓ cup creamy peanut butter	1¼ cups all-purpose flour
2 tablespoons margarine	¾ teaspoon baking soda
½ cup granulated sugar	¼ teaspoon salt
½ cup packed light brown sugar	1 tablespoon granulated sugar

Combine banana, peanut butter and margarine. Mix until creamy with hand-held mixer. Add sugars and egg; continue mixing until light and fluffy.

Add flour, soda and salt to batter. Use a spoon to stir until all the flour is mixed into the batter. Chill dough in the refrigerator for 15 minutes.

Drop dough by teaspoonfuls onto greased baking sheet. Sprinkle cookies with granulated sugar, then press a fork on top of each cookie twice to form a crisscross pattern.

Bake at 350° F. on middle rack of oven for 10-12 minutes or until golden brown.

Remove from baking sheet and place on cooling racks.

Prep: 35 minutes   Bake: 12 minutes   Makes: 36 cookies

Per Serving: 60 calories, 2g fat (0g sat.), 6mg cholesterol, 64mg sodium,
10g carbohydrate (0g dietary fiber, 6g sugars), 1g protein, 1% Vit A,
1% Vit C, 0% calcium, 2% iron, 1% potassium, 2% folate

Gingerbread Banana Cookies

2 ripe, small DOLE® Bananas
4 cups all-purpose flour
1 teaspoon baking soda
1½ teaspoons ground ginger

1 teaspoon ground cinnamon
½ cup margarine, softened
½ cup brown sugar, packed
½ cup dark molasses

Cut bananas into quarters and place in blender or food processor container. Cover; blend until mashed (⅔ cup).

Combine flour, baking soda, ginger and cinnamon in medium bowl; set aside.

Beat margarine and sugar in mixing bowl until light and fluffy. Beat in molasses and bananas until blended. Stir in flour mixture. (Dough will be stiff).

Cover and refrigerate dough for 1 hour. Divide dough into 4 parts. Roll each to ⅛-inch thickness. Cut dough with gingerbread man cookie cutter or other favorite shapes; place on greased cookie sheets.

Bake at 375°F 10 to 15 minutes or until just brown around edges. Cool on wire racks.

Prep: 30 minutes   Bake: 15 minutes   Makes: 30 cookies

Per Serving: 125 calories, 3g fat (1g sat.), 0 mg cholesterol, 81mg sodium,
22g carbohydrate (1g dietary fiber, 7g sugars), 2g protein, 3% Vit A,
1% Vit C, 2% calcium, 6% iron, 4% potassium, 8% folate

Banana Pudding

1½ cups sugar, divided
2 tablespoons flour
1½ cups evaporated milk
3 eggs
1 stick butter

1½ teaspoons vanilla, divided
3-4 DOLE® Bananas
¾ box vanilla wafers
¼ teaspoon cream of tartar

Mix 1 cup sugar and flour in a saucepan. Separate eggs. Stir yolks with a fork until blended. Add milk in same cup as egg yolks. Slowly stir egg mixture into sugar mixture until well blended.

Cook over low heat, stirring often, until a custard forms and thickens. Remove thickened custard from heat, add butter and allow to melt. Cool. Add 1 teaspoon vanilla.

Layer wafers and bananas in a 9x5x2-inch baking dish. Pour custard over wafers/bananas.

Add cream of tartar to the egg whites. Using electric mixer, beat until frothy. Continue beating and add ½ cup sugar and ½ teaspoon vanilla. Spread on top.

Bake at 375°F 10 to 15 minutes, until brown.

Prep: 15 minutes   Makes: 6-8 servings

To help bananas ripen, just put them in a paper bag with an apple or tomato. And to keep bananas longer, store them in the refrigerator. The peel will darken but, inside, the fruit will still be firm and delicious.

Banana Caramel Quesadillas

8 (6 inch) flour tortillas

¼ cup caramel sauce

2 cups grated Monterey
    Jack cheese, divided

2 green-tipped DOLE® Bananas

¼ cup margarine

2 teaspoons sugar

¼ teaspoon ground cinnamon

Arrange 4 tortillas on tray. Spread 1 tablespoon caramel sauce over each tortilla. Sprinkle ½ cup cheese over each tortilla.

Cut bananas into thin slices. Evenly divide banana slices over tortillas; top with remaining tortillas.

Melt 1½ teaspoons margarine in large non-stick skillet over medium heat. Place one quesadilla into skillet and cook until lightly browned. Add another 1½ teaspoons margarine and turn quesadilla; cook until lightly browned. Repeat process with remaining quesadillas.

Mix together sugar and cinnamon. Sprinkle over tops of quesadillas. Cut each quesadilla into 6 wedges. Serve with fresh fruit salsa, if desired.

Prep: 20 minutes Makes: 12 servings

Per Serving: 301 calories, 13g fat (5g sat.), 20mg cholesterol, 424mg sodium, 36g carbohydrate (2g dietary fiber, 8g sugars), 9g protein, 8% Vit A, 3% Vit C, 16% calcium, 9% iron, 4% potassium, 16% folate

Banana Jewel Cake

1 standard size box vanilla or white cake mix	2 tablespoons grated orange peel
1 cup water	1½ cups fresh cranberries
¼ cup orange juice	3 DOLE® Bananas, sliced
¼ cup sugar	

Prepare cake mix as directed, except add only 1 cup water. Pour into 13x9-inch baking pan.

Heat orange juice, sugar and grated peel in medium saucepan, until hot, stirring until sugar is dissolved. Add cranberries and simmer until skins burst. Add bananas. Continue cooking for one minute. Remove from heat.

Evenly spoon cranberry banana mixture over cake. Do not stir.

Bake at 350°F 35 to 40 minutes or until lightly browned.

Prep: 15 minutes   Bake: 35 minutes   Makes: 12 servings

Per Serving: 233 calories, 5g fat (1g sat.), 0mg cholesterol, 283mg sodium, 46g carbohydrate (2g dietary fiber, 32g sugars), 2g protein, 1% Vit A, 14% Vit C, 9% calcium, 4% iron, 5% potassium, 12% folate

Fresh Fruit Taco

3 tablespoons sugar
1 teaspoon ground cinnamon
4 (6-inch) flour tortillas
2 tablespoons water
Vegetable cooking spray
1 small box instant sugar-free vanilla or chocolate pudding mix

1 teaspoon grated lemon peel
1 teaspoon vanilla extract
1 DOLE® Banana, sliced
1 mango, peeled, sliced
1 kiwi fruit, peeled, sliced
½ cup raspberries

Combine sugar and cinnamon. Brush tortillas lightly with water. Sprinkle sugar mixture over both sides of tortillas.

Spray large custard cups with vegetable cooking spray. Gently press tortillas into cups. Bake at 400°F 10 minutes or until lightly browned. Cool.

Prepare pudding according to package directions. Stir lemon peel and vanilla into pudding.

Combine banana, mango, kiwi and raspberries in small bowl.

Arrange tortilla shells on dessert plates. Spoon about ½ cup pudding into each shell. Spoon fruit over pudding in shells.

Prep: 20 minutes Bake: 10 minutes   Makes: 4 servings

Per Serving: 248 calories, 3g fat (1g sat.), 0mg cholesterol, 485mg sodium, 54g carbohydrate (5g dietary fiber, 23g sugars), 4g protein, 9% Vit A, 66% Vit C, 6% calcium, 9% iron, 9% potassium, 14% folate

Banana Apple Betty

2 cups soft bread crumbs
½ cup packed brown sugar
⅓ cup granulated sugar
½ teaspoon ground cinnamon
2 firm large DOLE®
   Bananas, sliced
2 tart green apples,
   peeled, cored, chunked

¼ cup orange juice
⅛ teaspoon ground nutmeg
Vegetable cooking spray
3 tablespoons margarine,
   cut in small pieces
Frozen non-dairy whipped
   topping, thawed
   (optional)

Stir together bread crumbs, sugars and ¼ teaspoon cinnamon in medium bowl; set aside.

Combine bananas, apples, orange juice, remaining ¼ teaspoon cinnamon and nutmeg in medium bowl.

Sprinkle 2 tablespoons crumb mixture into bottom of 9-inch cake pan sprayed with vegetable cooking spray. Evenly spread fruit mixture over crumbs. Dot margarine over fruit. Sprinkle remaining crumb mixture evenly over fruit.

Bake at 375°F 30 to 35 minutes or until apples are tender. Cool slightly. Serve warm with whipped topping, if desired.

Prep: 20 minutes   Bake: 35 minutes   Makes: 8 servings

Per Serving: 192 calories, 5g fat (1g sat.), 0mg cholesterol, 116mg sodium, 38g carbohydrate (2g dietary fiber, 29g sugars), 1g protein, 5% Vit A, 13% Vit C, 3% calcium, 4% iron, 6% potassium, 5% folate

Fruit Dessert Pizza

1 pkg. (1 lb. 2 oz.) refrigerated sugar cookie dough
2 DOLE® Bananas
1 pkg. (8 oz.) light cream cheese
¼ cup sugar
2 tablespoons orange juice
1 pkg. (16 oz.) frozen peaches, thawed or
    1 can (15 oz.) sliced peaches, drained
2 cups fresh pineapple, cut into chunks
½ cup orange marmalade or apricot preserves
Mint leaves (optional)

Press small pieces of cookie dough onto greased 12-inch pizza pan. Bake at 350°F 10 to 12 minutes or until browned and puffed. Cool completely in pan on wire rack.

Cut one banana and put into blender container. Cover; blend until smooth (½ cup). Beat cream cheese, sugar, orange juice and blended banana in bowl until smooth. Spread over cooled cookie.

Slice remaining banana. Arrange banana slices, peaches and pineapple over cream cheese. Brush orange marmalade over fruit. Garnish with mint leaves, if desired.

Prep:15 minutes   Bake: 12 minutes   Makes: 10 servings

Per Serving: 394 calories, 15g fat (5g sat.), 27mg cholesterol, 292mg sodium, 63g carbohydrate (2g dietary fiber, 37g sugars), 5g protein, 22% Vit A, 110% Vit C, 20% calcium, 9% iron, 6% potassium, 11% folate

Bananas are more American than apple pie. In fact, this tropical fruit is the most popular fruit in America.

Banana Chocolate Mousse Parfait

¼ cup boiling water

⅔ cup semisweet
   chocolate chips

2 DOLE® Bananas
   (1 extra-ripe, 1 firm)

¼ cup packed brown sugar

½ teaspoon vanilla extract

1¼ cups frozen whipped
   topping, thawed

½ cup fresh or frozen
   raspberries

Pour boiling water over chocolate chips in small bowl; stir until smooth.

Combine extra-ripe banana, brown sugar, vanilla and melted chocolate in blender or food processor container.

Cover and blend until smooth. Fold in whipped topping. Spoon half of mousse into 4 parfait or dessert glasses. Slice firm banana over mousse in glasses. Spoon remaining mousse over bananas. Chill at least 30 minutes. Top with raspberries.

Prep: 15 minutes   Chill: 30 minutes   Makes: 4 servings

Per Serving: 313 calories, 13g fat (9g sat.), 0mg cholesterol, 9mg sodium,
52g carbohydrate (4g dietary fiber, 39g sugars), 2g protein, 1% Vit A,
15% Vit C, 3% calcium, 8% iron, 11% potassium, 4% folate

Index